DARKNESS [illegible] BOX

Michael Lloyd Bynoe

ARTHUR H. STOCKWELL LTD.
Torrs Park Ilfracombe Devon
Established 1898
www.ahstockwell.co.uk

First published in Great Britain, 2006

British Library Cataloguing-in-Publication Data.
A catalogue record for this book is available from the British Library.

Dedication:
To Anita

ISBN 978-0-7223-3681-6
ISBN 0-7223-3681-0
Printed in Great Britain by
Arthur H. Stockwell Ltd.
Torrs Park Ilfracombe
Devon

So Alone

I feel so alone.
I feel far gone.
It’s like drip, drip, drip
Of the brain drain.
I feel useless.
I feel sad,
’Cos this is the coldest day I’ve ever had.

Subliminal TV

Damaging our sanity,
Images of time replacing our mind.
Dark secrets disturbing our time.
All this information crowding our thoughts,
Driving our vanity to levels of insanity.
Self-help groups destroying humanity.
How long before we get old
And forget our real goal?

The Journey

When I saw you last night
You looked so sad and cold.
It was just that the night had got old.
I said, "Where are you are going?"
You said, "Somewhere in Hell."
I could sense your distant screams
Disappearing from this screen.

There was a flash
And the lights became dim.
I said, "Let me in, let me in."
Your flesh was burning.
Your mind was turning.
And then there was no sound
From the distance all around.

Move on Tomorrow

We’ve had enough of your abuse,
We have given all our lives,
’Cos it’s a crying shame whether we live or die.

How could we be ever equal,
When all our history has been deleted and humbled?
How could they sing about love,
When this love does not include us?

We’ve been controlled by the master’s whip,
Years and years of abuse and pain.
As time goes by, we’ve been tricked
In believing we are all the same.
It’s all been part of a generated game,
To drive our women and brains insane.
Let the truth be told,
Day after day we are still sold.
It’s all been part of a conspiracy
To keep most of us in jail.
So now the time has come
To get even, even tho’ we are on the run.

The Last Bell

Dragged screaming from the floor,
Through the clouds of an open door.
How long is this going to last?
'Cos it will be in the past.
As we open the gates of our mind
It will pass in the nick of time.
Open up our tortured soul,
This will be our main goal.
So how long is this going to last?
'Cos you don't need to look to the past. . . .

In Time

They bring ammunition
To knock down these walls.
We build the Promised Land.
All the people have saved our souls —
Now's the time for us
To achieve what's been sold.

Tired of queuing all our lives,
Parts of the world have continued our fight.
We've been granted freedom
But continue to serve our master's kingdom.
Time has moved on.
Still we toil from the shackles of repression
What's been part of our omission.

We pay our debts with death and fear
But tomorrow we will stand in the Temples of Glory.
Slaving away for our freedom,
Death and destruction
Will help us build our
Free Nation.

On the Beach

The weather in Rio is fine.
We go out and dine on shellfish, coke and wine.
On to the beach for fun and games
So we could go gaga and enjoy each other's pain.

What a shame!
What a shame!
Having fun in the rain,
Driving each other insane . . .
On to the beach for fun and games.

You

You make me nervous,
You make me sad.
You bring alive the dreams I always had.
You bring me joy
'Cos all my pain is destroyed.
I will always love you,
Even if you are thousands of miles away.
You are strong and would never go astray.

I stand condemned, thinking of you.
The pain, joy, the sorrow you've been through.
It's time to reflect on what's to be
And stand on the edge of time to see
What tomorrow will bring you for free.

It's a new day, it's a new year,
A bright future awaits you from here.
From the test of time
Be strong and cry
'Cos all you have to do is try. . . .

Now's the Time

Been rejected all my life.
Open the window of time.
Which way is it going?
When is it going to stop showing?
From the long and standing years,
Time has taken its toll
For something that wasn't my fault.
I've been the innocent one throughout all this
But yet I keep blaming myself.

Fighting against the tide,
Deliver myself on high
To the Saviour, who'll decide whether we live or die.
That's what kept me sane.
I came screaming into a world of shame.
What a joy to tell my story now,
'Cos my past was shrouded in secrecy and blame,
As another day goes by, filled with pain.

It's Your World

You hadn't told me
That you were leaving.
I only found out after you'd gone.
They used to say that you're
Living in a world of your own,
Filled with confusion.
Now the time has come to make a new start
And take it to your heart.

It's your world,
Do what you want to do.
It's your world,
Go on through and through.
It's your world,
Try and see what you want to be.
It's your world,
Between you and me.

You slip away in shades
From your world of familiar faces.
I understand how you feel.
Time after time will see you through.
As you stretch beyond the feeling of doubt
It casts a shadow to make you scream and shout.

Waiting

Sitting here on the sidings at Paddington,
A continued noise bellows through the station.
People milling around in their thousands.
Parts of this place are dark,
Parts of this place are bright.
The sun is creeping in along the lines
As another train prepares its journey on time.
People with prams, dogs, luggage, going crazy,
going abroad
To see Paradise in all its glory.

Times of Our Lives

I've been taking time out looking
At my life.
Day in day out
Just seems to pass me by.
Time would take its time,
You should know what to do.
With every roll of a dice you should know what to do.
Let me give you some advice to open up your heart
And show some emotions.

Times of our lives — times of our lives —
Times of our lives are going to change.
Times of our lives — times of our lives —
Times of our lives are going to change.
Whatever you do or say,
Dark or bright,
Times of our lives are going to change.

Why can't you understand?
When I take you by the hand
The shadow of darkness is going to fall.
Show me some emotions
'Cos I caught the light going down the hall.
Where are you going to run to
When the daylight's gone?

What is Life?

What is life?
If you are feeling this way.
What is life?
Leading you astray.
What is life?
Surviving from day to day.
What is life?
Picking up the pieces of broken fears.

I can't take this pain any more.
Instead, I'm going to head for the door.
Every day seems like a distant memory.
For every moment I stand and stare
From the processes that are here.

What is life?
Struggling to make it through the day.
The days which seem long and strange.
For every step we take
And every mistake we make.

Strange Love

Five days passed —
Haven't heard from you.
Thinking, talking and don't know what to do.
This pain is driving me off the road,
'Cos you are the noises in my mind.
Five days passed —
Haven't heard from you.
Thinking, talking and don't know what to do.
Smashing, smashing all my anger in vain;
Better be getting on the train.

Twisting and turning,
Then you leave me alone.
I just don't know what's going wrong
For your love has come and gone,
Like a cloud in the sky — in the sky.
Five days passed —
Haven't heard from you.
Thinking, talking and don't know what to do.
Wishing the time would come and go
So we could be together again.

The Morning After

Got up this morning feeling fine —
Just about everything on my mind.
I gathered my thoughts from the heart,
Struggling to make a brand-new start.
I switch on the television for the time
And it seems to control my mind.
I switch it off and find myself fuming —
Felt like a damaged human being.

I discovered this day, from the start,
Sent the pulses racing through my heart.
The day started gloomy,
'Cos this place is crazy, crazy.
It appears to get harder from here
But I'm minutes from life's Sad Café.

As I struggle with what's left today,
Changing times get stranger day by day.
The day is now hours old.
The skies get dark, angry and grey.
Another politician tells mechanised lies,
Positively telling us whether we live or die.
But what's left of today?
Maybe there's hope in this rotten decay?

The Free World

They spread their lies with propaganda
While the starving and dying scream and halloo.
They create wars
To annex the people's continent,
And inflict them with diseases
To control them like parasites.
When is mankind going to wake up
To this nightmare?
When is the Free World going to be free?
Free from the shackles of repression
Destroying the Rainbow nations.

Why Did You?

Why did you try to hurt me?
Why did you try to destroy me?
'Cos I uttered words that you didn't like
And acted somehow, creating a fight?
Or was it that you didn't like to see me having a fun time?

How could you be so calculated?
Grinding with anger and hatred.
This can't be right,
'Cos you are not out of my sight.

Filled with anger and pain,
Your loss is my gain.
Shedding light on this sad affair
You twisted the knife when I was far away.
Your dirty deeds
Are part of your Empire of Sin.
Your twisted mind
Is playing deadly games,
Whatever the time.

Still Lies Ahead

When you live in this life of sadness and misery,
Trying to make sense of these social diseases,
It gives you the feeling of total hopefulness
When all they seem to do is to leave us in a mess.
Each blaming the other for all this carnage
For all left destitute and dying.

We've travelled all these years
Along this dark and lonely path.
Which one is the right half?
We have fought for our freedom
But have been denied the pass.

Tired of burying all our lives,
Enduring days, months, years of strife.
Decades have come and gone, yet we are still
Fighting for what's rightfully ours.

The Final Exit

Driving my car at speed,
Trying to find a clear spot to
Carry out my deed.
The morning lightens —
At this moment I feel uptight.
The smell of burning rubber
Taking me deeper in my depression.

As the clouds grew angrier by the second
My thoughts became muddled and vague.
A voice in my head kept telling me,
"Do it now!"
My hands keep trembling
Asking me how
As the blood drained from my veins
I asked myself, "Is this a sin?"

The final hours slipping by,
Now's the time to say goodbye.
I slipped into a coma-like state,
Filling my mind with the pleasure of hate.
As the winds begin to whistle
The time has come for my final exit.

The Power Game

They play their games with toys.
They welcome a war.
When will the big fish learn,
What life is for?
People starving, dying everyday,
Creating death, destruction and fear.
When are we going to respect one another
Instead of playing political games for gain?

The great powers that be
Creating death, destruction for all to see,
While the Devil's doing his dirty work.
The powers that be plot the next invasion,
For an evolving world, full of confusion,
Where HUMANS distrust their own beings.
Now the time has come
For all to rise to this occasion.

Another Year

We leap into another year,
Trying to make sense of the one before.
Every day gets harder —
Every year gets darker.
Have faith in the one controlling our soul,
As we try to strive for our goals —
As we try to achieve our goals.

Another year —
Another year —
Another year about to start.
Now hope's from the heart.
Faith and dreams carry us through,
Meaning of life in full view.

Another year passes by.
I'm looking from the inside out (by and by).
We see the indifference of the human race.
Hating each other by or for the look on our faces.

A year has passed us by,
Where we beat the drum for the battle ahead.
Side by side —
Weak or strong —
We deliver the sacred, full of our endeavours.

Autumn

Autumn is here again.
Let's go for a walk along
The path of a damp day.
Look at the colours of the wild,
Trek through the bushes and tufted grass.
It's cold and crisp,
Looking at nature through the haze.

How beautiful is the sky,
Walking while we get high.
Surrounded by nature and lively wildlife.
Strolling along the path of a damp day,
Inhaling wonderful clean air,
Escaping from noises and pollution,
Getting lost in this evolution.